by Marilyn Hacker

PRESENTATION PIECE
SEPARATIONS

separations

separations

MARILYN HACKER

ALFRED A. KNOPF · NEW YORK · 1976

THIS IS A BORZOI BOOK
PUBLISHED BY ALFRED A. KNOPF, INC.

Copyright © 1972, 1973, 1974, 1975, 1976
by Marilyn Hacker
All rights reserved under International
and Pan-American Copyright Conventions.
Published in the United States
by Alfred A. Knopf, Inc., New York,
and simultaneously in Canada
by Random House of Canada Limited, Toronto.
Distributed by Random House, Inc., New York.

Acknowledgment is gratefully given to the following
magazines, in which some of the poems in this book
originally appeared: *Ambit, The American Review,
Arx, The Carleton Miscellany, Epoch, The Little
Magazine,* and *Stand.*

"After the Revolution" appeared in *The American
Poetry Anthology,* edited by Daniel Halpern,
published by Avon Books, 1975.

Grateful acknowledgment is made to Warner Bros.
Music for permission to reprint lyrics from "Rock and
Roll Heaven" (O'Day and Stevenson), page 4,
Copyright © 1972 Caesar's Music Library, Zapata
Music, Inc. & E.H. Morris & Co., Inc. All Rights
Reserved. Used by permission of Warner Bros. Music.

Library of Congress Cataloging in Publication Data
Hacker, Marilyn, [Date]
Separations.

Poems.
I. Title.
PS3558. A28S4   811'.5'4   75—36789
ISBN 0—394—40070—4
ISBN 0—394—73163—8 pbk.

Manufactured in the United States of America
First Edition

for Iva Alyxander
and for Luise

CONTENTS

GEOGRAPHER

GEOGRAPHER

for Link (Luther Thomas Cupp), 1947–1974

I

I have nothing to give you but these days,
laying broken stones on your waste, your death.
(The teeth behind kisses.) Nothing rhymes with death.
Richter plays Bach. My baby daughter plays
with a Gauloises pack. Once I learned pain and praise
of that good body, that mouth you curved for death.
Then your teeth clenched. Then you shivered. Seeing
        death.
Another of those mediocre lays.
Little Brother, of all the wastes, the ways
to live a bad movie, work a plot to death.
You worked your myth to death: your real death.
I've put my child to bed. I cannot eat.
This death is on my hands. This meat dead meat.

There is a cure for love. It is absence. There is a cure
for grief. (It is absence.) I cannot say,
you died, and I don't want to live today.
I fed my child. I learned to drive a car.
I went to work. The baby is in bed.
This is a formula I used before.
(I ate a veal chop.) Word, word, word: the cure
for hard nights. Somebody was always dead,
but not, certainly, you. You rattled speed-
ing, seven-thirty, through the door,
awash with daffodils. Did I stay
up all night drawing the bowl of fruit? I did.
And then we went to bed and slept till four.
You kept the drawing when I went away.

I I I

Sorry, I can't make any metaphors.
There is no talking horse. Billy the Kid
did what he did, and he died. Death is no mid-
wife birthing you to myth. You died, that's yours;
death is nobody, death is a word,
dying happens. People die. I will die.
You are dead, after five minutes of dying. Were you afraid? Last night I heard
of another poet dead, by her own hand
it seems (oh how I wish there were more
boozy women poets, aged sixty-seven:
new book, new man, wit and kitchen noted for
flavor). *If there's a Rock-n-Roll Heaven*
They sure have a Hell of a band.

IV

Metaphor slid in on the radio
like vision's limit; we see the night sky
a planetarium dome; mind, or eye,
won't take starry infinity, won't know
for more than a dawning shudder: I will die.
You died. Once, we walked along the beach
in the Pacific autumn twilight. Reaching for something, knowing you and not knowing, I
asked, were you afraid of dying. "No,
I don't know." I wanted to say how, lying in bed, I was ten, in the swish of cars
through rain outside, I knew, what you knew, and know
nothing now, that I was going to die,
and howled, hurled into the enormous stars.

V

This is for your body hidden in words
in the real city and the invisible city:
your words, Jack's, Hunce's, Lew's, Gerry's, my words,
golden scarabs, a carapace of words
crystalled opaque over your eyes, this death
that was your eyes. Hating words, I fumble words
into a bridge, a path, a wall. My words
are not to coax your saltiness this time;
they freeze you in this agate slice of time
where you would not be now except for words.
I am thirty-two. I have a child.
You were twenty-six, never a child

never a grown-up. At my feet, my child
puts a box in a bigger box, babbling almost-words.
You were eighteen, a smooth-cheeked, burning child,
black and gold on the snow where terrible chil-
dren honed the facets of the winter city.
I was twenty-three. I let you be the child.
Last century, I would have died in child-
birth, proving nothing at all in my death
except that women were duped, even to death.
I love my loud brave dirty woman-child.
She and I have gotten through, this time.
And you snuffed yourself out at the same time.

Bright in a frieze, the figures whittled of time
rescued from love and money, friends and child:
gem-lit bodies locked under my fur (near time
the Museum closed), we writhed, reflected; the time
we howled and rolled all night, elbows and words
gasping absurd (to get to work on time
we slept, at last, feet to head); the time
we mapped an imaginary city
on your graph pad. Shanghai, Leningrad, what cities
we pored over in picture-books, marking time!
Trite, how a lithe boy giving the slip to death
skips over maps, and one slip is, anyway, death.

Now I will be face to face with death
which has no face. I have had two weeks' time
to heft and weigh and hold and swallow your death.
I have written a lot of lines that end with *death*.
I have held your death the way I hold my child,

but it has no weight and it has no voice. The death
of a red begonia from frost, the hibernal death
of the Heath horse-chestnuts, colored, odored words
pile up. But I have not found the words
to thread the invisible waste of your death;
the quicksilver veins threading the map of a city,
till the lights all froze out, all over the city.

I am alive, in a grey, large, soft-edged city
you never saw, thinking of your death
in what is an imaginary city
for me. Once, I imagined a city.
You were born there. You took me there. In time
somebody might have thought it was my city.
Night after day after night, I mapped the city
on the brown geography of its child;
and the cliffs and hills and gemmed sky charted the
    child
like a wound flowering the streets of the city.
The wound clotted with jewels. The jewels were words.
I left you in the city, and took away words.

From the gutted building, we salvaged words,
raced down Nob Hill at midnight, bad child, bad child,
thinking we'd gotten away with it that time.
Past one now, and the night contains your death.
Now you have visited too many cities.

THE TERRIBLE CHILDREN

THE TERRIBLE CHILDREN

You, born half smothered in a caul of myth,
whose bursting heart was drowned in waves of sky,
salt-swollen on the scorching sand you lie,
bright flagellant beneath the whip of death.
You, who never tasted the fruit,
who woke wide and immobile in blue fire,
now, stretched to silence on the singing wire,
fall through limed fissures, naked, rigid, mute,
while summer children underneath the tree
gather the thick-dropped apples where they lie.

Hand in hand down snowcrusts, arrow-poised
arm folded under arm, dilated eyes
windows thrown open on a world of ice,
mirrors turned on an onyx checkerboard.
Their faces are not of brothers or lovers.
Blood never etched this congruence of curve;
no tie explains the way symmetric swerve
and flash of sound and movement ape each other,
nor explicates the bent, left-handed grace
their yoked forms sing, striding from place to place.

They fish the streets. A mirror is their net,
distorting human form before their pure
absurdity into caricature.
Politely offering dry hands and wet

smiles, words odorous as white hemp-flowers,
the gesture of a bow; a sudden turn,
they disappear. Against the sky they burn
in silhouette. And through the shrivelled hours
the others tread the inverse of their steps,
laughing, toe to long heel, till laughter stops.

The delicate purgation of a tongue
turned back over purgation: paradox
within a more intriguing paradox
of involuted mouth. The large eyes' long
panes reflect ritual violence
hung in a room apart, the separate
bright strands conglomerating intricate
woven patternings of death and silence.
The geometric flights of music, each
intoning a formality in speech:

If you are angle, I am complement.
If you are circle, I am circumscribed.
If my hands mold, yours is the form described.
Your voice is my familiar instrument.
I sound a note, and you complete the chord.
Your eyes are an inscription in my hand
that reads my face and tells me what I am.
My singing resonates beneath your words.
A move completes a move; as games are played,
if I betray, you are the one betrayed.

Crying ice tears, their faces washed in snow
till clean as knives, they walk through winter,
     wading
in frozen air. The moon is always fading
above them. Stars in intaglio
imprint a pattern on their upturned brows.
Loosely, their fingers latch. The star-seared mark
glows bloody effulgence in the dark.
Within the scarlet aureole, their mouths
cross, meet and linger, press to rediscover
the treacherous salt pungence of each other.

JEREMY BENTHAM IN GUANAJUATO

For myself, I would prefer to be alone,
savoring the privacy of my decay.
I cannot see a fraternity of death
beneath or above ground. Those without souls
should stay in solitude, to meditate
soullessly. There is a shame in death
when it is old and shared.
                              They've turned to leather.
Terminal wounds scream knives.
Their mouths are open too, in agony,
or in surprise, but calm now, even screaming.
Note that their genitals are gone. The organs
that formed them living abdicate for death.
You speak of flown souls; note these shriveled loins
that make a better line of demarcation.
Mother and child, soldier and priest, lover and lover,
have lost their stories in the lime museum.
Only, perhaps, a crumpled piece of parchment,
Ana Ramírez, dead in her first childbirth
tacked without ceremony on a belly.
And truly, I could not care less for stories
than for a name for each of the grey skulls

piled in the anteroom. Death has a lesson
for us, but not in tragedies and titles;
and these are here because they are
unpaid-for. Nameless now
they bear the better title of The Dead.
My presence cannot disconcert these objects.
(For such they are, and objects of instruction.
They, like the knife of Plato must be used
to fill a function well.) The end of man
is such. I feel some warped affection for them.
Indeed, I would not join their congregation;
these do not value privacy enough.
Sing in their chorus? No; I would prefer
to be alone
                    but why the mould and clay?
Dust soon enough, I'll do, alive or dead,
as I do best and speak as I still can.
We make a better audience than worms.

SEÑORA P.

Having no occupation and no child,
she gambles, and her mangy dogs run wild.
Dark-blown blond hair and party-practiced laugh
comfort and mock her from a photograph.
With charity bazaars, she marks the feasts
of saints, adores old actors and young priests.

THE SONG OF LIADAN

Liadan of Corkaguiney was one of the college of twelve bards of eighth-century Ireland, called ollaves. Touring the strongholds of the High Kings with her entourage of apprentices, she met and fell in love with Curithir, another ollave. He implored her to marry him. A son of theirs, he said, would be Ireland's greatest poet. She agreed to meet him after their rounds were finished. Later she had afterthoughts. Could love combine with the austerity of a bard's life? And why a son, and not a daughter? She rejoined Curithir, but only after taking a vow of chastity. He placed himself under the same vow, and the two went to live in the monastery of Saint Cummine. To avoid temptation, they were given the choice of seeing each other without speaking, or speaking through a crack in the wall and never seeing; poets, they chose speech. Liadan died soon after; Curithir went on a pilgrimage to Jerusalem.

I

A leaf in the path, a sere
finger of autumn, dust and a sway of branches,
dust and a rustle of death's muse,
blue and black a mantle under brown hair,
a sky, a wind, a note of the swineherd's song,
a step I did not take, a brown ash-
leaf in the path's dust.

My hair shall turn grey presently.
My hair shall be silver as the shocked moon,
my hair a web and my hands jewelled spiders.
I shall lie silver presently,
my hands leaves in the path, shadow fingers,
ice-caresses down the thighs of trees.
The swineherd flings acorns and apples in the
    afternoon,
roots and rich fungus in the afternoon,

dead flesh and offal in the afternoon,
devoured, mouldering into evening.

The sunlight etches runes over brocade,
two hands' electric juncture on brocade,
clasped fingers across pewter and brocade.
The swineherd sings. Soon my voice will melt to silver-
gummed webs clinging to the breaker's hand.
                                                  And I am silver
and barren.
Brocade. Our hands clasped in a truce of gauntlets,
a silence above song. Love would be
a myth of god's death, and my bright betrayal
scarlet and purple as a ceremony.

When I was seventeen, I loved a sailor
with sea-grime caked beneath his fingernails.
He taught me navigation and three tongues.
Later, I loved a scholar who spoke two.
My youth was bitter as a hard green fruit,
still bitter on the bough, and never ripe,
shrinking to dry core over a missed season.
Always, they say, gods have been born of virgins
who bloomed divinity, simplicity,
and warming pride. A child of mine
would eat fire, sing death, still my hands forever
with her uncompromised mortality.

Sing,
poets, girls, children. Unguents and incantations

to soothe the thighs, the lips, the hands, the eyes.
For a moment, dissolution. And the moon
bleeds. And the silver shot with
blood. And myself already scarlet,
falling, alive with imminent dying.

II
(First, the word,
    after the word, the cry,
    after the cry, the song.
    When will we know what we are seeking?)

You have imposed upon me a treaty of silence.
You have sealed my lips' stone with passion.
You have melted the speaking stone with your hand's
    heat
and your warm mouth is a band on mine.

There is a scream between us I have smothered.
There is a loud song frozen on the cold road.

My love is locked in a room without windows.
My ears are invaded by dissonant bells
sudden in cobbled silence. I cannot speak,
and in my body is a fear like metal.

A pendulum strikes on metal
and in my quick heart is the silence of bound hands.

The coming of spring is insidious and cruel.
The mist pervades my throat as it melted the crystal

my voice was. I am weak, and I much preferred
the hard agreement of our truce of gauntlets.

(Having the choice,
     the belly like a full fruit growing
     to burst and die, the sprung song-seeds
     sailing alive on blue air.)

     I I I
As the pulled root shrieks, as
the struck stone breaks, as
glass at a note-thrust
cracks, as
ice slivers from the sudden shard of spring;
cracked, broken, and slivered, shrieking
under the mad, sharp stars,
I shall dance, beloved,
and sing passion's reason to the blind walls.

     Nightingale, falcon and crow,
     Stand me witness to my vow:
     To be more and less than human,
     Perfect chord and barren woman,
     I will give my own heart's blood
     That my song may be renewed.
     Earth bewail and sky rejoice.
     Die, my body; live, my voice.

O saints that on the green earth trod
O Mary, got with child by God.

POEM FOR EDWIN DICKINSON

Painting, I make it harder than it is.
Look for the thing.
Center: interstice made by
her bent arm and belly, hand on thigh
tapered to acute angle, concave arc
of breast on top, behind. Behind is yellow,
blued with noon. The focus is her elbow
which has at least five colors: one is the green
her breast is splashed with;
three purples from her back; blue from the spine
meeting wall and shadows; highlights yellow; down the
    arm
salmon darker than the dappled thigh.
This bend draws colors. Draw.
See in the bent arm resting straightening thrust.
Shadows on the skin mean bone,
muscle curving the crook to wrap the forearm
crossing her far thigh at a lever's angle
lifting the upper arm, dark with heavy shoulder.
Behind is yellow. Sun and lemon
soften the crease from thigh to belly
and the back slope from waist to hip-bone.
Seeing, I make it simpler than it is.

CATHERINE

Star-cheeked Catherine has a catherine wheel
exploding on the velvet of her chest,
her smarting ribs pried parting by a spoke
of constellations shooting out on smoke
diagonal to darkness till she reels.
Level-limbed Catherine, child of circumstance,
propels herself into the winter dance
of frozen comets, lifts her head to mark
Orion straddling Fourth Street on the dark,
spanning the gutter with his studded limbs.
Catherine lifts her straining lids and swims
under the dazzled torrent of the sky,
darker than wide and half again as high.

CATHERINE IN LOVE

Her broad bones and green eyes from the Midi
reflected ocean in an infancy
of chilly longing. Looping wavelets broke
splashing his lips with bitter salt. They woke
in the familiar sunlight of a room
turned inland. Gold around her pupils reeled
into a wall of flame across a field;
his tongue touched lip, met cycles of salt spume.

CATHERINE PREGNANT

Eternal pressure shrinks the finite earth.
The waxing body swells with seeds of death.
The mind demands a measure to its breath
and in its convolutions comprehends
the endlessness in which it is contained,
the change that is its necessary end.
Change is neither merciful nor just.
They say Leonard of Vinci put his trust
in faulty paints: Christ's Supper turned to dust.
Winter dries the grass, freezes the dew.
Age may coin a lion on your brow
and stun my moving fingers with a blow,
while each expanding instant redefines
your face burned in my eyes with living lines.

CATHERINE MARRIED

Their child was born in March. Early in May
he watched her umber-dappled fingers play
in the north window spilling morning light
to get the prongs of ligament drawn right.

She would not work on canvas or on wood.
Near the mosaic coffee-table stood
a six-foot square of cardboard strung on wire:
farms in a starry valley, all on fire.

He tried to work. She yowled more than the child.
He couldn't teach her if she wouldn't smile.
Through June, her wide hands twisted in her lap.
She always smelled of garlic, or a trap.

Guests came to see his paintings. Everyone
turned to the burning valley. He was gone
most of the afternoons, sometimes all night.
His portrait of her glowed with leafy light.

Meticulously, with a paring knife
he cut the canvas features off his wife.
When he came back from taking down the trash
the cardboard valley strewed the floor with ash.

EQUINOCTIAL
for Bill McNeill

After the heavy-eyed boy usurer
reclaimed the prism he had dearly loaned,
scavengers took the carpets and the furs,
the crusted draperies nobody owned.
You packed your drawings in a cardboard roll,
wrapped the framed things in a pillowcase,
leaving the god cracked on the shower wall
whose mad benevolence had kept the place
alive that long.
            Spring hazard raises floods
and runs a roadbed through the kitchen door
where predatory witches track in mud.
Absence is a distance gone before.
Downstairs, the Rocky Mountains and the sea
imbue the air with possibility.

SOME OF THE BOYS

Scraggly goatee, Prussian moustache
salute each other with a clash
of steins against percussive noise,
in Sunday coats of clever boys
invoking demons in the zinc
basin of a classroom sink.
Repartee and studded leather
draw the sting of chilly weather.
Amyl nitrite and perfume
close the ceiling on the room.
On the carpet near the fire
silence motivates desire.
If the tapestry behind
the figurines is ill-defined
nothing has to be explained
to a body scarred and stained
by the excess of his own,
bruised, exhausted, and unknown.
Agate stare will not be placed
in a humiliated face,
measures the confining walls
as the onyx figure falls
below the cautious gilded frame.
He must look and see the same
drawn skin, nervous extremities
that the naked stranger sees.

BIRMINGHAM

Behind that music happening, they told him
"Never look at your face travelling.
Vision stops change."
The vision of his change: a doped rag
cloying his blind runnelled face
after the black melting from there to here,
purple moss over the glistening
surface of a foreign afternoon.
Measures these distances by tastes
tongued in mouths that speak another language.
Gold hands grope him with questions.
Long waxed rooms, guessed words
luminous on his eyelids. To be fixed
in this motherfucking indecision.
Homesick. Fear and an incipient
hardon. The voluptuous interpreter
breathes before that music, only heard,
and a fat child crawling across yellow kitchen tiles
stops and cries and the shaving mirror
of a few thousand mornings shimmers into tears
along with their tall story and he throws
his hand in front of his face to tear
this last long drunk. And breaks more glass.

SEPTEMBER

The umber dowagers of Henry Street
gossip from windows while they rest their feet:
The Jew on East Broadway sells rotten fruit.
Last night the cops busted a prostitute;
broke up a crap game in the hall next door—
woke up the kids at almost half past four.
As taken with the ripened fall of words
against the yard as what they saw or heard,
their voices scoop the sun like beautiful
harsh birds, until the cindered yard is dull
with evening, and the regularities
of grubby men and children home to eat.
Two laminated toucans pepper meat
as sunlight sheaths behind the sumac trees.

GODFATHER POEM

That Christmas Eve, my
godfather fed us pâté
de foie and champagne.

Later, he played the
piano and we waltzed on his
glossy parquet.

"It's very pretty,"
he said and turned the page, "but
your work won't get done.

Why should we watch you
preen, stroke and tongue each other
and play with mirrors?"

"Oh," I said, almost
missing a step, "but when I
was a scruffy, un-

gracious child, the first
thing you taught me was 'Whatever
happens, keep on dancing. . . .' "

AFTER THE REVOLUTION

There are different ways of dying without
actually dying. I was nineteen.
So was Milo. Pavel was twenty-two. The square
was hotter than this beach; the no-man's land
between July and October
when anything can happen
                      and nothing does.
They searched me. Nothing. They left me behind.
Every touch threatened; not the way a boy's
skin tingles to be touched.
                      If the gift leaves?
Might as well die.
                    I woke up with that line
and a bad temper. We waited
to see them on those balconies
as if they were girls.
                  I hardly know you:
an approximate age, oiled skin,
stones in the sun. We smelled each other.
Fear, yes. And, then, they had touched me.
So we waited. Are you a journalist?
I hope not. Why does it come down to
language? Pressures of bright air
over that other city; incipient autumn
swelled red and yellow skins. An instrument
incises the rough bark (feel it
signalling in the palm's crutch); thick sap
oozes amber marbled cream, the instant's
crystal, for the cabinet, crammed
with history. There are
unchronicled moments, the plane-tree

knifed on the air in the square court.
The boys waited.
        We waited.
                Dear friend; I am trying
to organize my expedition towards
the source.
        Every bedizened traveller
retailing gossip in the Market with
chunks of dark amber, angels enamelled on tin,
makes me think I can discover, if not
the actual "lake between three purple mountains"
above the falls, at least some old bachelor
with odd tastes, some witch's brat daughter,
who has been there, or claims it, and will show
(but not sell) a pebble, a dried herb
that smells like copper and quince. . . . If I do not
come back, if I disprove your theory
in a large-circulation periodical
or anything equally tasteless, remember
this note, and the token
I enclose.
        I will not be able
to lunch with you on Saturday.
                Sincerely,
Dear friend;
        Perhaps you will understand
when I say, I can no longer tolerate
this city. . . . No . . . The two young nuns
whom we watched strolling in the cloister
through the gap in the wall . . . if I said, their gait
seemed peculiar; if I added

the ostensible boy poet lodged
in what was Mother's room has got a pattern
to his intensities . . . I will not be
drawn into events that I cannot
control or understand. These things concern
soldiers, economists, geographers,
but I will not be made historical
by chance. Good-bye. Perhaps you know
more of this than I do, have considered
the possibility of my . . . retreat.
I must miss you on Saturday.
                              Yours faithfully,
Read it back. Tell me what I said.
                              Words.
The body's heavy syllables. Touch me.
Say. Nerves said, You will begin
to finish dying. The children are running away.
They are hiding in the gorse bushes. They
dribble your inner thigh. They are throwing
chocolate wrappers from the balcony.
What are they whispering? Tell me.
                              Milo remembered
a child on the beach, a fox-faced little girl
carving something from driftwood. It was late August,
early evening. He was nineteen. He gave her
half his cheese and two tomatoes. She was carving
an old woman in a shawl. Cheese brine
on her fingers stained the dry wood. Her hair
was cropped against lice, gold stubble on her neck.
I thought of touching her there. It was not

Milo, it was I. The salt still on her mouth.
Pavel had a stolen rifle. Milo
had an American pistol. You are not
a journalist?
                    I'm almost twelve,
she said. I already have breasts.
I can read French. I read *Madame Bovary*.
If they fire into the crowd, I said. I thought,
Pavel would be a handsome grandfather.
We are playing stupid games. I will kiss you, I said,
but I'll never speak to you again
if you tell anyone.
                    It flowered
his sweaty shirt-front. He crumpled, quizzically,
into the dazed heat. *"Pavel!"*
They searched me. Nothing. They left me behind.
A red ball sun plumbed the translucent water.
She lay on top of me, her knees
rubbing my trunks, her cotton shirt
damp and gritty on my bare chest. Licked salt
off my lips.
                    I looked for Milo for three days.
Dear friend;
                    It was once my language; now I can
barely read it. Even this note
may be written in code.
                    Yours in haste,
Here comes Pavel with lunch. The children
went crabbing with Milo and Douina. Don't
say anything to Milo . . . his job . . .
you understand. Not
as one might have wished.

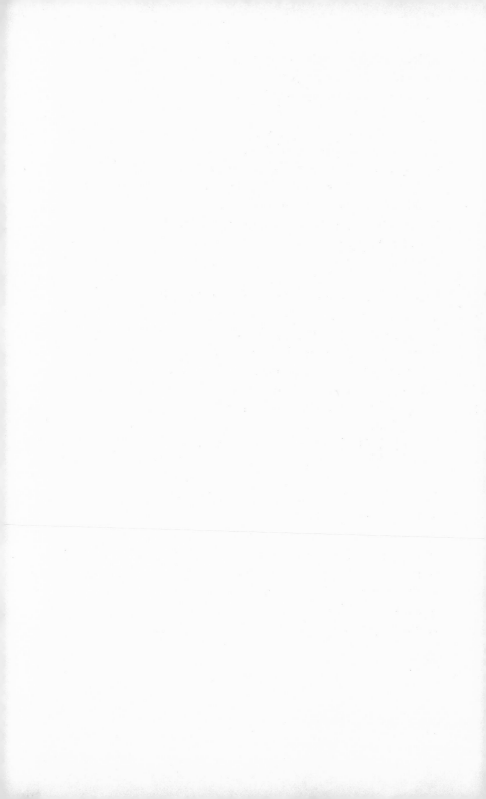

THE LAST TIME

ALBA: MARCH

Coming home to the white
morning light in my studio. Ten o'clock;
down the block construction workers stop
for coffee, beer, a drop of booze. It's cold;
they trample frozen mud. White
sunlight quivers in my head,
slivers in puddles breaking last night's freeze.
I finger keys in my woolly pocket, holding
a grocery bag striped golden with light.

All around the south windows
plants doze and shiver awake
as a new leaf breaks and uncurls. I unpack
a green enamel pot, black pepper, milk, eggs,
with the light melting my legs, like
that boy's long calves last night,
warm moons on my own
when we had grown drunk with kissing
stretched on slippery cool sheets.
I kissed his eyes, mouth, feet. I kissed his knees,
ate honey from the flower between his thighs
and felt it rise with sap against my tongue.
He was so young. His cheeks, as smooth as mine,
tasted of pears and wine, and that smile
was not for painters. While I held him
it swam above my drowned eyes.
Now I organize papers, inks, pens.
I'll draw the coleus again, its leaves
a curvilinear trap for light.

LIVING ON THE EDGE

Living on the edge
of a continent on the edge
of an ocean on the edge of a grinding
fault on the edge
of crossed blades, salt water dulling
the edge
            of the land breaking back into the ocean.
On the edge of calling him
by dream diminutives: Boychild,
Little Brother, she wonders, did he ever
mistake her for Mother, mistake her
sullen fits for murderous rage
remembering
the double thrust into
her in-
complete, red jewels
stabbing his eyes and outside
the soldiers have started
singing.
Certainly they distrusted
each other's dreams, when he began laughing
minutes before he woke, when she
struck out the back of her hand as her eyes
opened with tears.
                    And the old photograph
she kept on the edge
of a glass tray of turquoise
butterfly wings: he is eleven, she
thirteen, they are both kneeling, he
behind her, grabs

her shoulders, she has one arm across
her ribs under her teacup breasts, the other
reaches between her thighs toward his cock;
her head is turned, their open mouths glued.
The scene freezes. We will replay the scene.
Winds have shaped the small trees into
artificial unities. Outside the park
people are doing real things.
They wake up the landscape. Corridors
of eucalyptus over red-needled ground
arrange themselves around. "They smell
like the first time I slept with a grease monkey
and didn't know if I liked it."
                                The road
crosses the soccer field
down to the beach. A ruddy businessman
wrestles and races his blond ten-year-old.
The field is filtered green. The children scream.

CHAGRIN D'AMOUR

It is small
consolation that I can
remember more or less
all of the hundred-and-forty-seven-
odd times we fucked (I won't
enumerate; there are more productive
ways to suffer)
and the four hundred twelve (at least)
different faces you make still
asleep in the early
afternoon.
I had hoped
for a surfeit of your tongue
bringing my breath back afterwards. If
you feed a cat
liver for a while, he will get
really sick switched to other food.

SOMEWHERE IN A TURRET

Somewhere in a turret in time,
castled and catacombed in but
still on a tan street that
ends with a blue-and-white gingerbread house,
those rooms are still filled
with our pictures and books. On the sill
our black-and-white cat hums after a fly.
It is getting light. When we come in,
no one will ask you to leave, no one will send me away.

Nobody lives in the present, time
has textures past and future that
tongues taste at, fingers feel for.
The present happens in rooms
I am not in; past rooms
are only momentarily
empty, if I knew how
to turn around, I would cross the threshold smiling.
No one would ask me to leave, no one would send me
    away.

Don't think I'm trying to ignore the time
I piled my things into a cab and left
a note for you and one for the dinner guests.
Those rooms have new tenants. You and I
may never share a closet or a towel-rack
again. We contrived it. I am still

surprised waking up without you every morning.
But I can't camp out in your house or you in mine.
People would ask me to leave. People would send you
    away.

Still, I am an optimist. Sometime
we may be sitting, maybe near the ocean
on a cliff, and under the blown spray
get tangled in each other's fingers and hair;
and in that arbitrary future, your mouth
and the sea will taste of each other.
It is so easy to make things happen
like a freeze shot ending a movie
so you don't leave, and I don't go away.

But you know about words. You have had time
to figure out that hardly anyone
came back to bed because of a poem.
Poems praise and protect us from
our lovers. While I write this
I am not having heartburn
about your indifference. We could walk
into any room.
You wouldn't ask me to leave. I wouldn't send you
    away.

TWO FAREWELLS

I
Once, my
lovely, bedded in the almost-
dawn, you kissed me until I
came; it took perhaps
ten minutes, a most elegant
perversion.
And now you say
for years I have had
bad breath.

I I
"Try to turn
boys into men," Circe said,
"and they behave like pigs."

STONES, JEWELS

O hurry up, my guts convulse for love,
though I have only seen your neck, your wrist,
your lapis eyes worn underneath black lace.
You will be stone on me, remind me of
marble and amber, quartz and amethyst
while I taste my tongue corrode your face.
This lapidary passion for your face
could crystallize into a kind of love.
Your name drops from my tongue, an amethyst
pendant, carved into a hand and wrist.
Where are you? What will you be thinking of
later?
      I envy ladies draped in lace
who peeled and stared when they were all alone
till their own symmetry turned them to stone.

SONNET

Love drives its rackety blue caravan
right to the edge. The valley lies below,
unseasonable leaves shading the so-
seemly houses from the sun. We can
climb down. Cornflowers push from crevices
and little purple star-blooms with no name
we know. Look up. I didn't think we came
this far. Look down. No, don't. I think there is
a path between those rocks. Steady. Don't hold
my sleeve, you'll trip me. Oh, Jesus, I've turned
my ankle. Let me just sit down.   .   .   .
Predictably, it's dark. No lights go on
below. There is a dull red glow of burning at the edge. Predictably, it's cold.

RETURN

Sweet enemy, I can no longer
convince myself desire
is your diffidence, your beauty
is unkind, your excellent
long body scorns me.

You rise to me
without laughter or words,
too quickly beneath you I flower
open to what unknown
army.

Lying beside you I
dreamed I was lying
beside you, you smiled uncovering
my breasts, your hands in my hair, you
said "I love"

and long-haired
children lay on a green hill, we
walked past, journey-grimed, sweaty,
tired, we stretched on the slope
our knuckles touching

and their indolent
bodies rolled into a dance of
feathered serpents, sea blue,
sky blue, blue plumes in crystal
rain

around us. I
wanted to join the
dancers, seeding the sky for their own
pleasure. Girls and boys I'll never
bear you

crystallize
behind my knees, where you
once tasted, "I want to
know all the ways
of giving

you pleasure."
Serpents swallowed the rain,
grass, hill. We trudged a crowded
tropical city street; we had walked
for hours

looking for
your car, a room, some food.
Soldiers pushed past, speaking another language.
A dusty blue bus carried
the children away.

But when we
lay down in the yellow
wooden hotel bed, half-
dressed and thirsty,
we slept

knuckles touching,
washed by the hill-
magic we hadn't made;
first you smoothed my hair
and said

and I woke
beside your silence. Hunger
drew my mouth over you, urgent
and ashamed; companion,
adversary,

did we share
a blessing or elaborate
amusement at the infidelity
of vocabularies shared
by passing strangers?

IMAGINARY TRANSLATION

for James Keilty

These two meet for dinner once a week
in the old city. Middle-aged and grey
with some distinction—one wrote a verse play
that revolutionary students speak
intensely of; the other left archives
of an obscure study for politics,
talks urgency to Ministers and tricks
reason from hotheads—they lead public lives
of private circumspection, and they drink
together Thursdays. Twenty years ago
in a strange port, for two weeks and four days
they were lovers. Or enemies. They clink
snifters, wax quotable near 'Time,' then go
home their discrete and solitary ways.

SUGGESTIONS OF TRAVEL

At seven-thirty, omne animal
post coitum goes to get the car
repaired. Chastened toward chastity, you are
in an uncombed rush. I shall sleep more. I shall
get up still dripping you. Then a hot soak,
Pears Soap and Norinyl. Catch a noon train
north. Red eyelids and the linen stained.
Neither our mouths nor other quarters spoke
except of habit and chagrin. I'll stay
since I'm still here. August's annealing fires
subsumed on winter coasts. Tonight I'll read
in Manchester. Off then, packed all I need.
I wish we both were more accomplished liars.
I wish it wasn't going to snow today.

OCCASIONAL VERSES

"Your touch is abrasive. My blood seethes and smarts,"
said Sappho. Said Atthis, "Two pints and some darts."

"Stay," said Gaius, "it's keener than scandal when
    you—"
"I must go now," said Clodia. "The scandal was true."

"Your breasts are like melons, your mouth like dark
    plums,"
said Petrarch. Said Laura, "Why can't we be chums?"

"You move like a Phoenix on fire," said John.
"I'm off dancing," said Fanny. "You *do* carry on."

"Your glance is a torrent and I die of thirst,"
said William. Said Maud, "Revolution comes first."

"We're relations as well. . . ." Lytton coaxed Duncan
    Grant.
"We may *be* them," said Duncan, "but have them we
    can't."

I mull on poor poets who miffed their affairs
while you kip with the Muses discretely upstairs.

AFTER CATULLUS

*

Poems I wrote for you, in an
International Magazine!
After brandy I
showed you the proofs;
you handed them back
unread.

* *

Her father knew the major
dead poet's flatmate, tells a story
about his cook and a quivering blue blancmange.
She is more
interesting
for that. But the first-hand
article, not dead, not yet thirty,
coming at you
like a ten-ton lorry out of
control! If one runs me down,
sell my letters.

* * *

Tell him, Douglas, Virginia,
that all the lady novelists in
London can lay for him for all I care
and all New Bond Street spread-
eagle for his sad story.
This one poet who, unbidden,
sang him for everybody's children
will be silent.

GEODE
for D.G.B.

It is
from my landscape, and
is another landscape, a country
we never visited
together. I learned
enough of the language to buy bread,
fish, cheese, and wine. You made
friends with the old doctor, both getting by
with scraps of university German. (A coy
joke about parts of speech.) Brown-legged
children raise dust clouds on the one road.
The car door
was almost too hot to touch, and the seat covers burned.
A lizard flicks in the sand. We stood
breathless in that desert, the fleshy gems
full of light. I laid my flushed cheek
momentarily against your arm,
went on.
Inside the mouth of the cave
the jewels are wounded to speech.
They speak. The stones' wounds sing.
                              The surfaces hide
and surface in mutable light, facets
of smoky brilliance
to mass under a pale, veined column.
Hushed limbs shine

bluish, becoming gemmed,
other. No moisture;
the songs of the broken crystal
are clusters of crystals
that fork, accrete, erode.
                    The shaping
                    is painful, the enunciation
                    painful.
The object
stops, shimmering; struck to view,
it glistens, suggests something hidden,
rooted in cool onyx. Soothe
your forehead on stone. Never
is an adverb denoting time.
Listen. I tried to tell you. When the water
is gone, the crystals
still grow.

LA VIE DE CHÂTEAU
—a fiction

That morning, she crisply snapped a postcard
next to his cup. "I think this is for you,"
she said. *Bugger! How does that girl
know where I am?* "How does that girl know where
you are? Only my husband and the servants
know you've come here." "And the children."

"Is she in correspondence with your *children?*"
"Hardly." He smiled, rereading the postcard,
accepted through a swath of sun the servant's
proffered brioches, and more steamed milk. "*Are* you
going to explain?" Postcards fluttered from nowhere,
like the too-clever fingers of the girl.

It wouldn't do to think about the girl.
"I think that I'll go for a drive with the children
this morning." "I think that you'll go nowhere
until you explain." It was almost a rude postcard.
Well, quite rude. How *did* she know? How could you
explain one to the other? Now the servants

had left. He couldn't accustom himself to servants,
or didn't like to think he could. The girl
who ironed, dark and thin, an arrogant smile you
wanted to decipher . . . His children and her children
shouted in the orchard. He'd sent *her* a postcard,
of course. She hadn't sniffed him out of nowhere

with a very naked man headed for nowhere
running like hell (the older woman servant
sailed the plates off)—a British Museum postcard
of a Greek vase. "Let's forget that wretched girl.
I thought I'd have Françoise take all the children
swimming, and spend the morning alone with you."

"Yes, lovely, I'd like to spend the morning with you."
Blonde and blue air, a morning for getting nowhere.
Already he regretted the drive with the children,
regretted, really, consigning them to servants
on their holiday. Could they forget the girl
by lunch? He might send her another postcard.

"What are you looking at?" "Nothing. White lace. The
    servant's
apron." "I know where we'll go." Grappling the girl
like children in the dark. He'd send a postcard.

VILLANELLE: LATE SUMMER

I love you and it makes me rather dull
when everyone is voluble and gay.
The conversation hits a certain lull.

I moon, rattled as china in a bull-
shop, wanting to go, wanting to stay.
I love you and it makes me rather dull.

You might think I had cotton in my skull.
And why is one in Staithes and not in Hay?
The conversation hits a certain lull.

You took a fretful, unoriginal
and unrelaxing friend on holiday.
I love you and it makes me rather dull.

A sheepish sky, with puffs of yellow wool,
watches the tide interrogate the bay.
The conversation hits a certain lull.

And I am grimly silent, swollen full
of unsaid things. I certainly can't say
"I love you." And it makes me rather dull.
The conversation hits a certain lull.

GIFTS

Here. Between us I've placed a smooth stone,
green-veined, with finger-fissures, and a cracked
blue bowl with three yellow pears, and seven miles
of jagged coves, pebbled and bouldered, the jade sea
drooling and frothing them, one dwarfed tree,
a crooked surviving pine, on a tumbled cliff
lookout point. Hold the stone
in your palm, cold
from morning draughts on the window-sill.
The touched side takes your warmth. The cool
side rubs your lips. Your mouth
is on my hand.

RHETORIC

Friend, then, whatever has become of us
since each for each was the anonymous
stranger whose elusive qualities
as Other in the Dialogue more civilized
poets apostrophise?

Foundered on languages,
discovering each was another whose
perceived uncipherable difference frees
or limits, to get this far, just this far,
we have become precisely what we are.

THE LIFE OF A FEMALE ARTIST IS
FULL OF VICISSITUDES

Goes mad,
frescoes in shit on the walls;
cuddled and spoon-fed for
3 weeks out of the month, a
teeming resurrection in
oils thick as a sapling,
rough as a sycamore bole,
orange, blue, red, seventeen
shades of green, the crucified
woman burgeons to power.
Lucky if she doesn't
die of cancer at fifty-two, a
virgin, a lover of women they just once let touch one,
and her Muse,
bearded and placid, gets his wife pregnant again.

THE LAST TIME

Somebody has endlessly postponed
this summer; it is chilly and uncertain
as you, my own, not in the least my own.
I watched clouds move through the organza curtain
all afternoon. The noises of the farm
and loud birds ravaging Tom's kitchen garden
break on my book. Untrustworthy, the light
shifts every hour, wind sun fog sun wind storm.
I can't blame you, or ask your pardon,
or dream the day into another night

and wake up foundering between self-pity
and despair, the way I did today,
and take a morning train back to the city
where nothing much will happen anyway,
dubious individuals will write
dubious poetry, children will get cuffed
for nothing, and not forget it, I will fault
everyone fastidiously, tight-
assed and sceptical, obscure enough
to get away with it. O could I halt

this headfirst fall and rest love in your green
approval, tasting you like certainty,
summer would certainly start, something clean
and mobile as hill winds would move with me
and I would do . . . No, I do not believe
any of this, invoke it when I fear
the dull immobile speechless bland inert
mad lady who sits in me when I leave,
comfy as anything. Through her queer
nerveless hide, nothing pleasures, nothing hurts,

she could sit in the same place all day, all day,
not seeing, not hearing, not deaf, not blind,
her eyes like marbles and her flanks like whey;
the Sow reposes sated on my mind,
sated on what would have been a clean
if bitter lyric, setting me apart
from people who can say, "I did," "I thought,"
as real things. I have said what I mean,
more than I meant; and if I start
over, from the beginning, if she bought

my silence with that other fear: you will
always be alone, I will console
you, I would have to be still
or tell lies, if I believed in a soul,
damn it, if I believed in my art, fake
it. And I will believe in that,
if necessary, as an act of will,
and she, stuporous lunatic, makes me make
poems; more than love or fame, her flat
face presses inside my face; she spills

through me, hypoglycaemic languor
paralyzing rage, her rage, my rage.
Poles: pain and insensibility, anger
and absence, the senile queen, the murdering page.
He keeps me up all night. She makes me sleep
all day. Now clogged and vague, I maul the pain
to shape. They'll never let me out. Or I'm
not going. Anyway, not off the deep
end. Lovely people, I won't come again.
This is the last time. (That was the last time.)

PRISM AND LENS

PRISM AND LENS

Sour hemlock dregs and bitter love
have stained the sleepless rhythms of
the pale autumnal queen who pressed
bruised leaves of broom between her breasts.
The boys of spring, their heads turned south,
with yellow flowers in their mouths;
their laurel arms and butter knees
are sucked down pristine vortices
of life that lies and death that soars
and love that breaks the lips of scars
and with inquiring fingers grinds
fresh salt into forgotten wounds
as time's equivocation locks
its knuckles on the equinox.

These nights old madwomen chant in the streets
wailing their deaths to the October dusk.
Precocious cold sullies our gelid sheets.
Our hands turn yellow, and a sticky crust
devils our eyelids wakening. The husk
of absent harvest, pallid, skyborne, beats
a shadow sheaf into the window dust.
The rats wax bold without enough to eat.

I have no cognizance of what you feel.
What do you know of me? I am alone.
The turning sockets on the rack of bone
rotate like the cogged hubs of jointed wheels.
Synaptic sparks strike from them as they run.
Beneath the water's glazed excrescences

the slow unfolding of anemones
implodes a phosphorescence on the sun
as sound breaks on the silence of the sea.
A slight deflection of the middle ear
cracks the reflected sky. I cannot hear.
Sound shatters on the long hush of the sea
as we wake on the crumbling sand, the black
landscape of dreams outlined behind our backs.

God, but I hoped the night would never end.
Still, the moon faded, and encroaching light
fingered the purple darkness into corners.
You hoisted up your coat over your shoulders,
prodding the crumbs of morning from your eyes,
closed the kitchen door softly behind you,
sleep still webbing your eyelids to their rims,
loped past a stray dog cowering on the stairs,
crossed the cold hall, opened the broken door.
It was still very early in the morning.
A calendar torn in the alleyway
washed the pavingblocks with scattered days.

Turn a familiar corner, autumn rust
limns the pavingstones with burnished scales.
A sudden shift of focus: waiting just
around the corner, just where focus fails
to mesh, the shifting point at which you must
abandon sight, a shaft of light impales
a widened shadow with a single thrust
blinding the eyes that you have ceased to trust.

11

She howls home late on strange October nights
in a hunter's jacket over a soiled pullover
with pockets full of desultory objects.
The pocked lascivious moon brings down her blood.

My mother got me awfully overdressed.
This fellow took me over in a cab.
He had red skin. His big hand, like a crab,
fumbled through my collar at my breast
and then completely disarranged my hair.
I felt three hairpins fall inside my coat
and tangle in the muffler at my throat.
I don't recall exactly who was there . . .
a boy with an emaciated face
who drank can after can of lukewarm beer
and turned away if anyone came near
or walked away to a vacated place
or took more beer from the refrigerator
and gulped it loudly on the windowsill.
"You shouldn't drink it if it makes you ill,"
I said, and he would not speak to me later.
A dark-haired girl who had the slightest lisp
who came wearing a man's blue flannel shirt
and sneakers that were decadent with dirt.
Her eyes were mellow, though her voice was crisp.
She sat off in the kitchen with a book.
I came and sat beside her, just by chance,
because I felt too out of place to dance.
Her eyes were lucent amber, when I looked.
She struck a match, and over the round flame

looked at me with a sort of open smile
that said I ought to stay and talk a while.
I happened to have overheard her name
and knew that she had been in school with X
who was, in turn, a friend of Y and Z
who were at least on speaking terms with me
so I announced myself. She looked perplexed,
then didn't look perplexed and didn't care
and talked of something trivial instead.
I saw a couple on the sofa-bed
writhing, and attempted not to stare.
I guess she saw me looking at the floor,
was quiet for a moment. Then she said
something that made me turn and lift my head.
I don't remember what though anymore.
I don't know what I said. I wish I could
remember that. Once, I stretched out my hand
and stared at it and hoped she'd understand
and tell me what I never understood
but that was what she never understood,
although I tried to say, and wasn't able.
I let my hand fall on the kitchen table
and spread my yellow fingers on the wood.

III

In the chill outer rooms of strangers' houses,
women's rearrangements or men's disorder,
with nothing that remains to do but wait,
chafing rough cold palms between the knees,
sometimes watching a corner of the ceiling,

sometimes watching a small obtrusive spider
skeletize a silken polyhedron
from a remoter corner of the ceiling.
Someone is waiting in the other room.

　　We sit in a cold room. A. pours the tea.
　　A gaudy twilight helps us hide ourselves.
　　I try to read the titles on the shelves
　　and juggle cup and saucer on my knee.
　　A. tells me anecdotes that I have read.
　　I poise a studied ambiguity.
　　A. wonders will I turn my head and see
　　the crumpled blue kimono on the bed.
　　I pick a crystal ashtray up to watch
　　its slow rotation slap a waterfall
　　of iridescent limbs across a wall,
　　fumble with cigarettes. A. strikes a match
　　as the enormity of darkness swells
　　upward in a cacophony of bells.

　I V
　I will not lie and say I spent the night
　calmly, ate a light meal, washed my hair,
　read novels with hot coffee by my chair,
　then brushed my teeth, undressed, switched off the
　　　　light.
　I came back twice to see if you were there,
　and, when you weren't, left, hoping I might
　walk off your absence, or walk off the tight
　fist closing on my gut and cease to care;

but first I left a note that said I'd gone
walking, and I turned the lights all on.
The glancing lamps reflected my wet face
uncomprehending in a tight grimace.
I walked across the city in the rain,
river to river, then walked back again.

The sun drops quickly. Night rips the green sky.
Pale flares of incandescent mercury
drop limpid pools along the broad expanse
where shadows scatter in a jagged dance
on broken pavingstones and frozen tar,
and scarlet flashes break the flight of cars.
Dull gold in dim rooms, figures pause and pass
naked between a prism and a glass.
The lamps along the river, one by one,
spear the dark wings that hover on the sun.

Darkness and moisture settle on my cheeks.
The rain dissolves to close mist in the air.
(You sat back rigid in the easy chair,
your fingers gripped the arms. You would not
    speak.)
The fog thins out in front of me, revealing
careening grillwork on a tenement.
(You told me then. I wondered what you meant.
A flake of plaster crashed down from the ceiling.)
The shape of movement comes before the act,
contorts the face into a score of faces,

converts each possibility to fact.
A host of orgiastic angels come
trod me with spurious equilibrium.

v

Someone is waiting in the other room.
Someone is waiting just across the street.
Someone is waiting just beyond your sight.
The conversation comes to an impasse.
Something that ran in breathless from the cold
turns dry and measured as the hours grow old.
Word meshes word. The walls have turned to glass.
As the long instant of a touch ignites,
blurred shapes, whirled into focus by his fears,
plunge headlong down the chasm of the years.
The passing night remembers other nights.
Precluding sleep, a blanket of unease
falls on spent thighs and interlocking knees.
You shift your shoulder and avert your face
from the circumference of the embrace.
He thrusts his hands under the pillow, tries
to break the mirrors hung behind his eyes.

Here is the hub of ambiguity.
Electric spectra splash across the street.
Equivocation knots the shadowed features
of boys who are not boys; a quirk of darkness
shrivels a full mouth to senility
or pares it to a razor-edge, pours acid

across an amber cheek, fingers
a crotch, or smashes in the pelvic arch
and wells a dark clot oozing on a chest,
dispelled with motion, or a flare of light
that swells the lips and dribbles them with blood.
They say the hustlers paint their lips with blood.
They say the same crowd surges up the street
and down again, like driftwood borne
tidewise ashore and sucked away with backwash,
only to slap into the sand again,
only to be jerked out and spun away.
Driftwood: the narrow hips, the liquid eyes,
wide or thin shoulders, smooth or roughened hands,
the grey-faced jackals kneeling to their prey.
The colors disappear at break of day
when stragglers toward the west riverdocks meet
young sailors ambling shipward on the street.

You learn to know a city by its rivers,
crackling cellophane under the sun
or heaving rubber on a cloudy night,
what kind of boats haul cargo down to sea
or tug the moorings or patrol the banks,
what bridges leap across in transverse flight,
what kind of boys go prowling on the docks
or fish on Sundays with their paunchy fathers
or flash naked in summer from the pilings.

Two cops in a patrolcar came
and stopped me by the riverside.
They asked me my address, my name,
and had I thought of suicide.

"I came to watch the morning rise."
They stared in a peculiar way,
and one, appearing very wise,
said there would be no sun that day,

and girls should not stay out all night
and roam at random in the park
where deeds too warped for human sight
were perpetrated in the dark,

and midnight cold and morning chill
are detrimental to the liver,
and I had not convinced them still
I would not jump into the river,

and did not seem to be of age
for wandering at break of day
and would incur parental rage,
or else might be a runaway,

or else had fled a husband's house
to finish a nocturnal fight,

confounding the bewildered spouse
in stationhouses all the night.

"I may go drifting anyplace,
lawful and with impunity."
The headlights' glare upon my face
suggested my majority.

And when the streetlamps flickered, I
leaned on the rail and spoke no more
and watched the morning open high
bright wings across the Brooklyn shore.

A boy stood on the broad rim of concrete
that rims the churning river (this was down
a mile nearer the sea-tip of the town)
walled in on either side by empty piers.
Waves on concrete crashed thunder in our ears.
I watched him from the rain-slicked cobbled street
where sun-shot oil glistened like melted butter
and jutting shapes were coated with maroon
thicknesses of early afternoon.
A gull above the pilings circled three
perfect arcs, then headed down to sea.
The wind expostulated in the gutter.
I saw him stretch his open hand out, twist
it in again, clenched in an awkward fist.

Without shifting his feet, he turned his head,
acknowledged that he knew what I had seen.
I said to him, "Who are you?"
                              and he said,
"You know my name."
                              "That isn't what I mean."
My voice was booming underneath the rush
of water and the roaring in the sky.
His voice was still and clear within the hush
of echo.
        "I can tell you who, not why."
Not why my back impinges on your eyes,
my reaching hands impinge upon your hands.
My face wheels to the water and denies
your lengthened shadow falling where I stand.
Over the river wash, a seagull cries
against the wind, and hovers nearer land.

THREE SEASONS: 1944

for Baird Robinson

Squeezing his eyelids shut, he hears the squeak
of splintered pineboards in the cabin floor
as musky tropic winds finger the door.
Above his head, the white inverted peaks
of netting tacked around the metal cot
glimmer like sticky chrysalids. He thinks
he hears his parents laughing and the clink
of veined green glasses at the bar. A spot
back of his neck is itchy, and he shifts.
You see the Main House just across the lawn?
You're big now—almost five. We won't be long.
He scratches, and the slow white netting drifts
down—to smother him. He blinks, and yells,
thrusting his hands in front of him. Nails ratch
against the web that billows round to catch
his nose and mouth in gauze before he falls.
Eyelids and lips scratched to soft white that clings
like something foul, he sickeningly swings,
tangled out of the bed, above the floor
as singing cloys the air beyond the door.

Clanking a copper chatelaine of keys,
the school director told what he would teach.
Late summer woodlight splotched across their
    knees.
His mother's cheeks were mottled like a peach.
The shingled porch was flocked with silver beech
that made him think of pond-ice, cloudy cold.
The lintels were two arms beyond his reach.
The other boys looked serious and old.

They'd been flown out of England, she had told
him in the car, most, orphaned by the war.
He bit his nails and she began to scold.
"I'm glad that I won't see you anymore,"
he said, banging his elbow on the door
and waiting; but she didn't say a word
and then went on with what she'd said before.
But he had whispered, so she hadn't heard.

The warble of an unfamiliar bird—
he looked across the driveway with surprise.
"Young man, I don't believe you heard
a word we've said!" He rubbed his moistened eyes.
Against the sky, the spiring tops of trees
circled him into darkening filigrees.
The afternoon was busy. First he tore
his cuff on planter's wire behind a vine.
He hoped the house had attics to explore,
but those were dorms. He told a boy on line
about St. Croix, and when he would be nine.
The first-form proctor barked a reprimand.
His mother's day-dimmed taillights passed the sign
fronting the lawn before he waved his hand.

At first he missed his mother and his bike.
He had already gotten to connect
her absence with two aunts he didn't like
and Grandmother's disdain. He didn't expect
this other lack, muscular and direct.
(It was six months since he had learned to ride,

pushing off, wobbly, from a wooden block
eight times; then sudden balance, speed, and pride.
As if he had forgotten how to fly,
he fantasized, dawdling behind a book,
doing tight figure eights he hadn't tried
across his father's lawn at Sandy Hook
where he had never been since he was five.)

All the forty English boys had been
down in a low-beamed cellar, damp and black,
pressed, arms and belly against clammy back,
while sirens ripped the oilcloth shades. Between
the whine of bombers and the strafing guns,
each had decided that if anyone
should scream, or piss himself, or start to cry,
or chuck his food, there was no reason why
this should be remembered later on
upstairs, after the Jerry planes were gone.

The second time, two outbuildings were hit
and something made big potholes in the lawn.
The Board decided to evacuate.
A day before the third raid, they were gone.
The insular porched building in Vermont
held them no more than the flashed memory
of those five days; and by common consent
they didn't mention that. The foreign trees
saw troop-drills, though, and on the dorm walls
        scraps
of colored page approximated maps.

Exile was a schedule that they kept
whose order helped them regulate their fears
to days. Sometimes sweats broke while they slept,
but there were no blue tantrums, and no tears.

They found him young, and backward for his years,
too small, and still too scrawny for his size,
indifferent to their rituals upstairs.
At first they looked at him to clarify
the long grey hills that stared down their grey eyes,
but he was not impassable, nor stern,
and left them ample freedom to surmise
if he were stupid, mad, or taciturn,
so quick to understand, so slow to learn,
with lips and pointed chin of a tame fox
watching a rumpled winter sparrow turn
in flight from frosted tree to glaze-blurred rocks.
Once, someone found him hiding past the rocks,
pencil in blue-nailed fist, chewing his lips,
drawing on a salvaged cardboard box
the last of three tall-masted, web-rigged ships.
Most of the time he fumbled, though. He stuttered
and blushed in class when called on to recite.
He dropped tossed balls as if his palms were
        buttered
and never got code-words or answers right.
They watched him ominously when, at night,
clasped palms between his knees, knees drawn to
        chin,
he waited, lumped with blankets, for shut lights

to draw down darkness between him and them.
Perhaps if they had ever caught him in
some somber evocation in the sheets
like theirs, they would have jeered, then taken him,
proving Sin seaworthy. But he was chaste
for them, and more than chaste, lay still,
and more than still, lay rigid, as with fear
of what he might do if he moved, although
no one had shelled *his* cellar that past year.

There was a gable in the roof, from where
the exiled boys, with brass binoculars,
kept watch, by turns, for bombers in the air
and never watched the gravelled drive. Some cars
would rattle up: the postman in a jeep
with sparse mail for the teachers; headlight beams
at night—the doctor's Ford. Someone can't sleep.
Recurrent fever, or recurrent dreams.
One night he had a clear, disturbing dream:
a class held on the porch. His desk and chair
were third in the fourth row. It didn't seem
surprising that his books and pen were there
when he sat down. The rest, all standing, stared.
He woke wanting to cry, and hide, and cry.
The picture snarled into a knot and snared
under his ribs. He didn't remember why.
He hid in doodling. Four days spiralled by.
The weather was unusual for March.
Carpenters came. Since it was warm and dry,
they moved the first form math class to the porch.

The line of boys in shorts filed on the porch.
Smallest, he stood in front, studied his feet.
White light blazed broken shutters like a torch.
He went to the fourth row and took his seat.
His books were in the desk. He heard the neat
voice calling roll and places, then his name.
"Who told you where to sit?" The prickly heat
flushing his neck was almost fear, then shame.
Clasping his chilly fingers on his knees,
he watched the pink circle of faces freeze
into the iris of closing trees.

THE CALLERS

Pads in a quilted bathrobe to the door.
Today, she is a psychiatric nurse
tending the woman on the second floor
(chronic obesity) who has perverse
fantasies that lurk in corners, squat
beneath rouged lamps. Beyond the door are three
tall cutouts in the blinking sunlight that
stand forward as she clicks the peephole. She
pads in thermal quilting to the door,
counting the slap of mules from stair to stair,
as migraine repetitions lace her, bore
needleholes where her name escapes. Thick hair
like hers falls on the dark brow of one
boy whose hands hesitate towards her. A son
of hers, remembered with a cue
for swellings and excuses. Every year
brought the bloating and another new
wrinkled disappearance.
                              "Why are you here?
Your counsellor should come this afternoon."
"I haven't had a counsellor for years,
Mother."
              "Of course you have. He'll be here soon,"
and turns, and lets them follow her upstairs.

Squat in the reddened corners of the room,
shadows fidget in adrenal haze.
She keeps it twilight while the afternoon
light bars the windowframes against the shades.
Hulking from the sofa, Walter stands

toward the ceiling, darkening the wall,
quakes and sits when they offer their hands
to him.
      "Walter, this is my son, Paul."
"I'm not Paul, Mother. I'm Thomas."
                                  "Oh,
Thomas, your brother Paul is sick.
Sunday he was arrested. Do you know
Walter, my fiancé? It's so thick
in here, but I know I'll catch cold
if I open the windows," feels the chill
and tugs her sleeves down, wondering how old
he is now.
      "Raymond, Emmanuelle,
my mother."
         The man and woman near the door
come forward, smiling and severe.
New foster-parents? What have they come for?
She wonders if they want to leave him here.
They shake her hand, sit in opposing chairs
in corners like good children washed for tea.
She licks her flaking lips and pats her hair.
"Thomas, why don't you ever write to me?
I'm working as a psychiatric nurse
you know, two afternoons a month.
I had a breakdown, you know. That's the curse
our family must live with. Everyone
has problems, that's what I always say.
Like my brother's drinking. Walter here
was my patient. He feels bad today.
We're getting married when he's well, next year.
No sense in rushing, is there, that's what I

always say, no sense."
                    The room is bright
enough to hurt her eyes.
                         "Mother, why
was Paul arrested?"
                    "Last Saturday night
he stole ten dollars from a grocery store.
He works there afternoons, you know. He did it
for attention. I can't control him anymore.
He spent it all on candy. He admitted
he took it, to Miss Watson at the Home
he lives at. Sit there. Haven't I lost weight?"
They mustn't all look at her. Valium
calms them. Two fingers tap eight
palm-doses.
                    Thomas squats on carpeting
in the fringed pool of a lamp, Emmanuelle
above him on a straight chair, fingering
the frayed cuffs of her suede jacket. Well
out of the light, blue-eyed Raymond cracks
his knuckles softly, softly, staring
at the line of Thomas' half-turned back.
Beside her, Walter's thick fingers are tearing,
crushing, rolling cellophane. She takes
the pack of cigarettes away. Today
she drops his dosage. Apprehension makes
a sweet taste in her mouth.
                         "Now will you stay
in town a while? How long have you been here?"
Darkness climbs the ladders on the wall,
menacing the ceiling. They appear

restive this evening. She must sweep out all
the corners. Thomas is a wicked boy
to run away from home. His mother takes
the kitchen knife and four pink pills today
for nerves. What is he saying? Her headache
is coming back. Inside the china cage
cracking behind her forehead, something blots
on the carpet. He was forward for his age.
Drips on porcelain forget-me-nots.
Compose the hands. "You know your grandmother
is dead. She went mad before she died.
She always asked for you. Always. Your brother
was away. You can't escape it, that's what I
always say. Last week your uncle called
but I hung up. That man is not allowed
in my house. My doctor says that alcohol
promotes mental decay. He said that now
I can treat myself, that's what he said,
write my own prescriptions."

                    Walter prods
the sofa-cushions with his fists and spreads
his knees.

      "Good health is a gift of God,"
and God will punish sinners. Thomas was
evil like her mother. They would talk
about her in the other room, play cards
and laugh.

      "I've got to go now." Walter works

his way up to an undetermined height
and tracks his shadow to the door.
                                    "Good-bye.
You'll come to dinner here on Sunday night."
He goes.
            "He's very sick, you know. He's my
patient."
            Thomas, near the woman's knee,
widens his dark eyes through vermilion shade.
"He's always been extremely kind to me.
Now we can talk, Thomas. You must stay
when Paul's counsellor visits. Will you write
to Paul? I'm too nervous now, you know.
When Betty-Mae gives me my pills at night
she writes letters for me sometimes. Do you
remember Betty-Mae?" He nods his head
out of the puddled lamplight. Ashy dusk
fingers his smooth cheeks like, as if. Instead
of chicken, Betty-Mae could do a roast
on Sunday. Suddenly she feels
bloated, floating on her back in thick
sweet syrup. No cheating between meals,
the doctor said. Downstairs, somebody knocks.

Counting the careful steps down to the door,
she plucks the robe out over her belly. They
must not be left alone too long. One more
—what—she lost count of. But today
she is a psychiatric nurse. Her hands

realign the medication tray
to allow the doorknob. A brown man
with a brown briefcase and a grey
suit:

    "I'm from the Youth Board, ma'am.

                        Your son
is on my case file."

              Once again the blaze
of unfamiliar sky charring the dun
figure before it.

        "Well, come in."

                She stays
fixed on the threshold, swaying with the street,
until he is above her on the stairs.
She turns, eyes full of ashes, with the sweet
taste in her mouth. Walking behind, she bears
herself as though her abdomen were big.
A nurse can't do that though, because it looks
bad for the patients. She wonders if her legs
have swelled. Ahead, the Youth Board worker walks
into her parlor, passing Thomas where
he watches from the doorway.

                "Hello, sir."
"Thomas, isn't it? What are you doing here?"
"This is my mother," standing next to her.
"Well, now you're out of our hands." Near the door,
Thomas hunkers on his heels again
between the strangers, as the counsellor
walks to the couch. Pleasant to have nice men

for tea. "May I fix you some tea?"
"Thanks, I have other visits. I can't stay."
He opens up the briefcase on his knees.
"Our work comes first, that's what I always say."
He looks at her, and smiles as she sits down
beside him.
                    "Your son is at La Honda Ranch
for Boys, about a half-hour's drive from town
If he does well there, he has a good chance
of coming home soon. I have photographs
to show you, of the building and the grounds.
They live better than we do, there."
                                        He laughs.
"One day you must come out and look around."
In a mottled cardboard frame like lace
are five pink stucco houses in a row,
each of whose door and windows make a face
like in a picture-book her long-ago-
gone father gave her.
                        "Your boy will be in Section A
for six weeks, kept to grounds. In Section B
he can come to the city for the day
twice a month, on Sundays."
                            "Can I keep
the picture?"
            "If he does well in Sec-
tion A, he goes to Section B
after six weeks. Otherwise he is kept
in Section A. You can come to see
him, and the grounds, on any Sunday."
                                        "I

can't leave the house. I haven't been well. Now
I'm going back to work. I am a psychiatric nurse, you know. How
is he doing? He's mentally ill,
you know."
                    "No, no one told me. . . ." Pad and pen
appear. "Mrs.-uh- you'll have to tell
me about this."
                    "He's been sick since he was ten.
His records are with the Youth Guidance Board."
"I'm with the Board, ma'am, and I haven't seen
evidence. . . ."
                    "My advice won't be ignored
as a professional."
                    "I haven't been
free to see your son. You may be right."
(At a gesture from Emmanuelle,
Raymond takes out cigarettes and lights
one for himself, for her, for Thomas.)
                                        "Will
you be able to provide a car
for the boy to come and visit you
on his free Sundays? In six weeks we are
transferring him to Section B where two
home visits monthly are permitted."
                                        "No,
I can't afford that. I don't drive.
My brother drives, but he is not allowed
in my house. When my mother was alive
she drove."
                    "I see. Well, perhaps you can call

another parent. I suppose you'd like to know
when Thomas will be coming home."
                              "Paul,"
softly says Thomas from the carpet.
                              "Oh,
yes. Paul."
         "He isn't coming here.
He never lived here. He was at a Home.
He was happy there. They know him there.
He should see a priest. He is a Ro-
man Catholic."
                   "I see." The ball-point dips
as she picks up the eggshell cardboard stand,
traces pink houses under her fingertips
and presses it collapsed between her hands,
flat as a filing-card. Paul is away,
and he will get a paper cup and pills
tonight at bedtime. Downstairs, Betty-Mae
is fixing supper. God the Father kills
the sinners' children. Thomas must not stay
past dark. Is it already dark?
The painted children rise outside.
                              "Good day.
Call me if you have questions."
                              Is the mark
already on his forehead? Thomas rises
with the stranger.
                   "You should cut your hair,
Thomas."
         He blocks the lamp, revivifies

arachnid dark congealing under chairs.
They go out on the landing. Who will dance
in lapping spotlights on the street tonight?
Raymond looks toward the doorway, rubbing his
     hands.
Emmanuelle, smoking in the lamplight,
lifts her head and smiles. They both smile,
and Thomas insubstantially returns
like something that will move a little while
and then be still. This hunger, how it burns
under her heart. It's almost suppertime.
The three are standing, Thomas facing her,
a glowing shape on either side of him,
cutting scorched paths back to where they were
sitting. They can't come for her here. She lives
here. Everything went so well today.
She was a Nurse. She'll tell them she forgives
Thomas. . . .
                    "Mother, we have to leave."
                                        They go
      away.

Alone, she tours around the room three times,
checking the placement of the figurines
and china cups. Behind the crystal chimes,
she finds the seven caps of Thorazine
she hid from Betty-Mae. Out of her sleeve,
she takes the picture of the Ranch for Boys
and sets it on the mantel. Streetlights weave
the wall. She draws the drapes to dull the noise.

THE COMPANION

Everywhere you are coaxing the mad
boy into your room. You offer him
cold meat and beer. You light the fire
or the stove or the electric grate.
It is always cold. The winter city
solidifies under pale sun. The street
is full of little knots of gossiping
men. He crouches on your narrow bed,
cracking his knuckles in his lap. His hair
is dirty, falling in his eyes. His eyes
are muddy, fixed on you. You sit
cross-legged on the floor next to the grate,
chain-smoking, eating a yellow pear
down to the core. It is all gone. What will
you say to him? He has nothing to say
to you, staring at his large red hands. He is
not real. His baggy olive corduroys
are frayed through at the knees. You watch his knees
for some fraternal gesture. Now your face
is sweating. Every pore glistens with oil.
His cheeks are pocked. He knows about your dream.
There is nothing he can tell you, but you watch
his arms, his tense neck, scrawl an alphabet
older than birds' teeth on the patchy wall.
He is evidently used to ladies
alone in patchy rooms, used to ladies
who come home from work and staple tapestries
no one will ever see on the blue ceiling
above the bed, used to ladies
with plants, cats, paintings, Gordon's Gin and pills.

He has no double. Objects come in pairs:
shoes, lamps, gloves, couples dining at tables
for two, policemen, telephone repairmen, nuns,
sailors on leave. But you and he are no
pair. Peach-stone of solitude, he is
cracking his knuckles in your head, suggesting
only what you told him, drinking your beer,
eating your words, eating your sweaty hours,
bargaining eyes for time, trading his pain
for your sleep, all without a word
you can remember. You will look for words
in his ears, under his chewed nails, between his livid,
thin shanks. You will look for words
accrued behind the posters on the wall,
clogging the sink-drain, in the frying-pan
sticky with last night's curry, in a glass,
an ashtray, a green sock under the bed.
Objects crawl with words, rupture their pairs,
pile up between you. He gets easily
drunk. You too. You are my family
after all, pouring on the gin,
little brother, enigmatic cousin,
mother's sky-blue boy. Must every lover
leave you here, demanding plastic screen
of what an everyday good lady wants?
No lover though, no novel, no landscape
intimating frenzy. Curtains and walls.
He leaves. Next morning you are on a train
nearing the sea. Rose dawn beyond Marseilles
and 5 AM awakenings are normal

on trains. Perhaps it was his dream
you forgot this morning; vision of
your mind, a cheesecloth or a teastrainer
that nightmares filter through. Midnight gut pain,
cold tiles, boots, darkness, to the john next door,
then lying in the morning garden, under
a cherry tree, faint whining of a loom
inside the house, a leather-cheeked old man
with a blue beret, hunching for violets
in the next field. I tricked you, Little Brother,
enclosed you in my belly. I will not
produce you here. Little Brother
waits after dinner in the outlanders'
cafe, drinking a marc and Schweppes,
looking like that Austrian émigré
with the peculiar eyes. You leave your friends
stroking each other's knees and gossiping,
to sit with him. He still has nothing
to say. The thick white saucers
pile up. You lean against the heater.
Last Saturday, one hundred forty-seven
adolescents burned to death, clawing the nailed-
shut fire exit of a thé-dansant:
Grenoble. The kids shout in the room next door,
drinking beer and roasting chestnuts, dancing
badly. They have the elegant thin bones
of Leonardo angels, last year's slang.
Most of them are fourteen. Little Brother
is hitchhiking to Carcassonne. One boy,
pale as a mushroom thinking a blonde moustache,

rests his clubbed right foot in a workhorse boot,
reversed, against the bar rail, watching.
What makes you think a cripple ought to know
any better. Sentimental bitch.
And goes, and you rejoin your friends. You wish
your train would come. Tomorrow your train comes.
You wish some enterprising sorcerer
would save a niche in his pentangular
observatory for you. Angular
and shy in the muse's naked outfit, he
enfolds you in the corporeal star
where Little Brother, scarlet in your head
and smug, still can't prank swords into your bed.
The train curves up abruptly from the sea
and you veer up from your unlikely wish
into a windowful of scenery.
I'll bring the loaves, my old. You'll fry the fish.
It's L.B. come to keep you company.
Was that your pincushion under the seat
last night? Silent before, now garrulous;
you wish he'd shut his face and put his feet
down. Mais quelle gueule! Built like a bus
you are, and with a face like runny cheese
this morning. Pitiful. Cat got your sleep?
The Dijonnais truck-salesman plants his knees
on either side of yours, leans forward. Keep
two conversations going, c'est pas chouette.
You could do without both, and watch the rilled
blade of the Rhone cut valleys. Etiquette:
answer, smile, don't throw things. Have you killed

your mother yet? Boys weaned on paradox
bore me. Go away. He goes away,
leaving the commerçant in purple socks
leering. He's kept that leer on since Marseilles.
He left you alone in Venice. Silent,
as the grey water slurped the dirty white
carved landings, you rode the vaporetto like
other tourists, watching the hollow stage-
set city retreat to Tintoretto's age,
or Byron's, more nostalgic, less remote.
Scummed winter water nibbled on the boat
shoring at the Ferrovia where you
present yourself again at almost dawn
for drizzling Florence in the afternoon.
Now, in another room, you see yourself
putting a bowl of milk beside the door,
hanging up garlic from the moulding, learning
Greek. You could be crouching by the fire
with an unopened book, again redoing
your last spoiled scene, washing your hair again,
washing the dishes, washing your face, bemused in
your own bad smell. Instead you set
a pint of bitter and some sandwiches
out on the coffee-table with your borrowed
typewriter. Everywhere you are
coaxing him into your room.

SEPARATIONS

SEPARATIONS

I

Satisfied lovers eat big breakfasts. I
want black coffee and a cigarette
to dull this cottonmouth. Nine-ten. The wet-
faced construction workers hunkered by
the Pioneer Grill grin as I walk past.
You tried to be sleeping when I left
your room. The sweaty blanket hugged the cleft
between your buttocks. Now a crowd of fast
clouds scutters across the cautious sky
above the Fillmore West. We didn't make
it this time. Maybe it will take
another year. If you still want to try.
We try, and fail again, and try, and fail.
I'll be back home an hour before the mail.

II

Girl we describe most littoral to life
of sliding surfaces, the nectarines
and Nordic peach live more within their means
in yellow wicker than you do. Not wife,
lover or mother, incidental friend,
scrabbler for fame, income uncertain, form
too strong in verse, too weak in body. Warm
oversoon and oversprung to bend.
Instruct me in the compass of my knees,
say I, and when was I last rude
to whom, who since has firmly shut the door?
I mean, love me and I will listen for
your voice, do not and your carpings intrude
on my direction. Pointed as I please.

III

I'm putting words into your mouth again
instead of toes or fingers, breast or tongue.
I lust after my lust when I was young,
specific tastes of unspecific men
on definitely seasoned afternoons,
and chewing on the certainty of fame
arriving at multisyllabic-named
places, suave and polyglot and soon.
And the nostalgia of the underripe
for episodes when they were even greener,
and perpetrated ambiguities
on hairy kids for amorality's
sake. Now the confusion is deeper, leaner,
but after-imaged with the same-hued stripe.

IV

And underneath a phthisic honesty
shivers I gave you all this, I, I,
the undernourished fishy female cry
on learning muses don't get royalties.
Words like the dripping faucet in the sink
erode familiar runnels in my brain:
I like being alone and I like pain.
I'm safe clutching old feelings when I think.
The open oven hisses at my back.
I linger in the kitchen, warm as soup,
and will not walk across town to the bar
where homosexual barbed poets are
repeating confrontations in a loop
circuit gossip will edit and play back.

v

This is a high and sprawling wooden flat
with seven rooms, three tenants, and four beds.
We all nurture each other in our heads
and keep our distances outside of that.
Each cares for his own plants and his own cat;
we all like gossip, magic, plots and food
and spending half a day on last night's mood
or conversation or delicious brat.
We all are vague with anger and affection.
I love them both, and not for power or sex,
and if they love me I am fortunate,
and if they love each other they'll debate
themselves; but we have saved each other's necks
for risking in more challenging directions.

v i

I still balk at my preference for rhyme
which hounds me like an inarticulate
and homely lover whom I wish would wait
outside; no, he can meet my friends this time,
screw vanity, I love him, he's my own
obsession. Voice: you clever girls and boys
may hear a kid stomping and making noise
because she's scared left in the house alone.
I set the midnight table for a new
unfledged muse, my dream-wounded animus
whose boots scuff up the stairs now. Angular
child, I have to tell them who you are,
and love you so much they will envy us
and want you so much they will want you too.

VII

I'll dabble in specifics in my bath,
fingering soap and dirt off pinkened skin.
"Someday when I'm notorious and thin,
supple in love, magnificent in wrath . . ."
Someday when I'm a lady nearing thirty,
who diets and has not had sex for weeks,
acne and crowsfeet fighting for my cheeks,
I'll wish my mind, and not my feet, were dirty.
I lean back in the tub, but now it's not
hot enough. I scrub my soles, and wish
Manhattan midnight steamed outside, and I
could go out coatless while the smoggy sky
simmered a river dawn of oil and fish
to take a walk with you. I can't. Now what?

VIII

I don't count up days of your absence; they
are of two kinds, either alike or not.
I do the same day's work in the same spot,
sun slanting on the desk across the bay
window, and stop for lunch when Brodecky
gets up; we talk, how was the bar last night,
what's in the mail, more coffee, was I right
about him, I always thought, did she?
Sometimes I go out later, or I feed
guests, and if I'm lucky, we converse.
It wouldn't be much different if you were
here, because you aren't living here.
You'd come, we'd talk, feel better, or feel worse.
You'd leave, I'd go to bed, alone, and need.

IX

Most circumspect good friend, if, by "deceive,"
you mean keep secret who is in his bed,
trust that name, age, etcetera, were said
collect over Long Distance. I believe
in Higher Gossip, shifting states of soul
revealed in nervous tics, beer and bons mots:
what do you think he thinks, I want to know,
and feels, and is maintaining in control.
And I am fairly confident that he
would also want to know that sort of thing,
at the most cynical, because he craves
reassurance I still misbehave.
O Doubtful Thomas, stop malingering
and tell me what he's saying about me!

X

You're on the telephone from far away,
and we talk money. Meaning love, or food?
You disapprove of me. I think I should
not have to lop off blackmail from my pay.
I don't like taking handouts, and I don't
like you turning something I have earned
into a handout. Maybe I have learned
I'm competent. I'll make it, or I won't.
I'm burning with displeaseds and disapproves.
Let's fight like lovers if we have to fight
and gouge these holes from rage or jealousy.
You mean to hurt, and you are hurting me,
not drafting texts on what is good and right.
I am in pain, but I am still in love.

X I

I struggle up from sleep into the foggy
morning, grey again today, the grey
routine of absence permeates the day.
I shove the pillows off. A dialogue
continues that was started in a dream
where you were scolding me for being cold
to someone. Bath. The poems are not cold.
Coffee. It is trivial to scream
forever. Later I must write to you.
We go to North Beach to rehearse the play.
I fix myself a sandwich and a drink,
arrange the desk for working, while I think,
"Three weeks from now this will be far away."
The doorbell rings. The night is something new.

X I I

And if my compass straggles to your chest's
ferrous tangle and I dock again
seaworthy on your salt, love, lave me then
gently of seagrime. Hold me and let me rest.
Inquire where the erosions and the scars
come from, and if I am cradled well
out of the wind, I possibly will tell
the truth. While my conceit consults the stars
to navigate, I, not metaphor,
am informed by distance. You become
this journey, as eye-sockets define
vision. Distance finishes the line
and shapes a destination for the poem
while I plot courses toward a human harbor.

XIII

The letter that I want to write to you
is problematical for me to start.
I try to gauge how far we are apart
and see a vast parenthesis. The blue
sky tautens behind the morning haze.
The mountains will be visible by noon.
Downstairs, the twins make applesauce and croon
French songs they learned at camp. In four more days
I'll start out for Toronto on the train.
Two cities more, then one for both of us,
and then, as Alice said, "I'll be too far
away." It frightens me to think you are
two weeks away. We will have to pass
carefully. And separate again.

XIV

Friend (this is an imaginary letter
to someone I don't know), out of the hewn-
rock mountains, with the muddy morning rain
raising steam on spring-pools (but a scatter
of snowfields on the peaks), the train descends
to prairies looking shabby under storm
blankets. I am eating bread and cheese
to stretch two dollars out over three days.
(Vancouver was extravagant.) I'm warm
jackknifed under my fur. The train's growl blends
with nightsounds of old men, babies, a plains-
woman's beery laugh. Legs cramped, I go
to sleep, rocked by a Cree kid's radio
wailing blues' soulsolace on the night train.

X V

And here we are, or rather, here am I;
hungover, headachy, insomniac.
The clock rings four. I turn onto my back.
Four-thirty. Five. Wet traffic whispers by
Thamesward. I've been in London for
twelve hours now. It's already getting light.
I sit up, take my notebook, try to write
ten reasons not to see you anymore.
One: you will hurt me; Two: you will resent
my hurt; Three: but I light a cigarette
and sit against the wall and smoke instead,
thinking of times I've been kicked out of bed
and suffered O. Tired, as the curtains get
pale, I write this, and sleep all morning, spent.

X V I

Culled from the brambled ceiling of my wide-
eyed latternights, he spends the afternoon
across the room, quiet at first, but soon
proffering novels about suicide
and madness in instructional detail.
This is the way it's done. Watch every crack
in the soiled wall flap open and coax back
your eyes to where I stand, a limber, pale
absence. Dead woman, you are not my twin;
why do we have a brother, following
me to foreign cities, saying: make
words, make noise, make time, tonight you'll wake
staring in halflight, sweating, lingering
under my cold suggestions on your skin.

Only constant in his absence, he's
month-faced as Mother, face turns into face
into an alphabet of features, piece-
meal, reconstituted mysteries
served up for supper on a heavy plate,
cracked down the center with his morning smile.
The trains clack like a drummer out of style;
the gas-red ball slides down the chimney. Wait
beside the heater, thumbing through a stack
of crumpled papers on financial schemes.
Numbers drop to the rug; strands of loose hair
drop to the rug; an eye, a thumb, an ear
pile desultorily between my knees. It seems
none of the faces will be coming back.

X V I I I

A February of the merely real,
plumbers, not bayonets, outside the door,
colds, personal despair. I wrote, "The war
is far away," back to Perine Place reel-
ing and sick with tear-gas from a taut
poets-cum-journalists' soirée. The shades
were drawn. We joked about the barricades,
listening to gunfire. I got caught
by a bugmask's canister on Haight.
Sinecured exiles with unfunny eyes
converge on the Cultural Attache's
free whisky, playing Corner Points for praise.
It's hard to tell the poets from the spies.
The war is far away. Will wait. Will wait.

Marilyn Hacker was born in New York City on Thanksgiving Day, 1942, and was educated at the Bronx High School of Science, Washington Square College of New York University, and the Art Students League. She has lived in New York, Mexico City, San Francisco, and London; briefly taught; briefly sorted mail at the post office; edited paperback novels, a men's magazine, engineering trade journals, a poetry magazine, and a quarterly of speculative fiction; and been an antiquarian bookseller. She has one daughter, Iva Alyxander, two years old.

A NOTE ABOUT THE TYPE

The text of this book was set on the Linotype in Palatino, a type face designed by the noted German typographer Hermann Zapf. Named after Giovanbattista Palatino, a writing master of Renaissance Italy, Palatino was the first of Zapf's type faces to be introduced to America. The first designs for the face were made in 1948, and the fonts for the complete face were issued between 1950 and 1952. Like all Zapf-designed type faces, Palatino is beautifully balanced and exceedingly readable.

The book was composed, printed, and bound by American Book–Stratford Press, Saddle Brook, New Jersey.

The typography and binding design are by Camilla Filancia.